CELEBRATING THE NAME HANNAH

Celebrating the Name Hannah

Walter the Educator

Silent King Books

SILENT KING BOOKS

SKB

Copyright © 2024 by Walter the Educator

All rights reserved. No part of this book may be reproduced in any manner whatsoever without written permission except in the case of brief quotations embodied in critical articles and reviews.

First Printing, 2024

Disclaimer
This book is a literary work; poems are not about specific persons, locations, situations, and/or circumstances unless mentioned in a historical context. This book is for entertainment and informational purposes only. The author and publisher offer this information without warranties expressed or implied. No matter the grounds, neither the author nor the publisher will be accountable for any losses, injuries, or other damages caused by the reader's use of this book. The use of this book acknowledges an understanding and acceptance of this disclaimer.

dedicated to everyone with the first name of Hannah

HANNAH

Hannah, a beacon of grace and light.

HANNAH

With syllables sweet, like whispered breeze,

HANNAH

In poetry's embrace, she finds her ease.

HANNAH

From ancient lands to modern day,

HANNAH

Hannah's presence finds its way.

HANNAH

A melody of letters, a dance of sound,

HANNAH

In every verse, her name is crowned.

HANNAH

In gardens fair and forests deep,

HANNAH

Hannah's name, a promise to keep.

HANNAH

Each bloom that opens, each tree that sways,

HANNAH

Echoes her name in endless praise.

HANNAH

In tales of old and stories anew,

HANNAH

Hannah's essence breaks on through.

HANNAH

A heroine strong, a muse divine,

HANNAH

In every narrative, her name will shine.

HANNAH

In the symphony of life's grand scheme,

HANNAH

Hannah's name, a recurring dream.

HANNAH

A symphony of consonants and vowels,

HANNAH

In every stanza, her name enshrouds.

HANNAH

From dawn's first light to twilight's fall,

HANNAH

Hannah's name, a timeless call.

HANNAH

A beacon of hope, a guiding star,

HANNAH

In every journey, she travels far.

HANNAH

In oceans vast and skies above,

HANNAH

Hannah's name, a song of love.

HANNAH

Each wave that crashes, each star that gleams,

HANNAH

Whispers her name in endless streams.

HANNAH

In the tapestry of time and space,

HANNAH

Hannah's name finds its place.

HANNAH

A thread of fate, a stitch so fine,

HANNAH

In every pattern, her name entwines.

HANNAH

In the gallery of life's masterpiece,

HANNAH

Hannah's name, a work of peace.

HANNAH

Each stroke of color, each stroke of line,

HANNAH

Paints her name in shades divine.

HANNAH

In the quiet moments of the night,

HANNAH

Hannah's name, a guiding light.

HANNAH

Each whisper heard, each prayer said,

HANNAH

Carries her name, a blessing spread.

HANNAH

So let us raise our voices high,

HANNAH

And sing of Hannah to the sky.

HANNAH

For in her name, we find our grace,

HANNAH

A timeless echo in time's embrace.

HANNAH

ABOUT THE CREATOR

Walter the Educator is one of the pseudonyms for Walter Anderson. Formally educated in Chemistry, Business, and Education, he is an educator, an author, a diverse entrepreneur, and he is the son of a disabled war veteran. "Walter the Educator" shares his time between educating and creating. He holds interests and owns several creative projects that entertain, enlighten, enhance, and educate, hoping to inspire and motivate you.

Follow, find new works, and stay up to date
with Walter the Educator™
at WaltertheEducator.com

www.ingramcontent.com/pod-product-compliance
Lightning Source LLC
LaVergne TN
LVHW012049070526
838201LV00082B/3879